Roses

A Wisley Handbook

Roses

MICHAEL GIBSON DHM

Cassell

The Royal Horticultural Society

 THE ROYAL HORTICULTURAL SOCIETY

Cassell Educational Limited
Villiers House, 41/47 Strand,
London WC2N 5JE
for the Royal Horticultural Society

First published 1989
Second edition 1990

British Library Cataloguing in Publication Data
Gibson, Michael
  Roses
  1. Gardens. Roses
  I. Title
  635.9′33372

ISBN 0-304-32003-X

Photographs and line drawings by Michael Gibson

Design by Lesley Stewart

Phototypesetting by Chapterhouse Ltd, Formby
Printed in Hong Kong by Wing King Tong Co. Ltd

Cover: the superb large-flowered 'Paul Shirville' blooms with
the abandon of a cluster-flowered rose.
p. 1: 'Peaudouce', a tall-growing large-flowered rose with
blooms of show quality.
p. 2: the large-flowered 'Silver Jubilee' is very floriferous
and reliable.
Back cover: 'National Trust', a large-flowered rose which is
excellent for bedding.

Contents

The flowers of the Gallica 'Charles de Mills' are typical of many old roses with their densely arranged petals

Roses old and new

Because of their incredibly wide range of sizes, of flower and leaf form and of habit of growth, roses are perhaps the most versatile plants in the garden. The uses to which they can be put will be dealt with in the next chapter (p.12), but to make full sense of these it is necessary to know something of the different groups which allow such versatility. Brief descriptions follow, in historical order.

SPECIES OR WILD ROSES

The flowers of the wild roses of the United Kingdom are too fleeting to make them good garden plants. However, there are many species from other parts of the northern hemisphere, particularly the Far East, which bear their flowers over much longer periods, often followed by ornamental hips, and have decorative foliage. They are big bushes in the main, with long, arching canes taking them up to 7 ft (2.1 m) or more and as much across. A few, such as 'Canary Bird' and R. × harisonii, come into bloom in May or even April in a good year.

OLD GARDEN ROSES

These include the Gallica group, the Damasks, Albas, Centifolias, Moss roses and Chinas and, apart from the latter, flower only at midsummer. They vary greatly and sometimes it is by no means certain to which group a particular rose belongs. Owing to cross-breeding among themselves in the wild and later in nurseries (before it was realized that hybridization was something that could be carried out deliberately by man and not simply by insects or the wind distributing pollen indiscriminately), the boundaries between one group and another have become blurred. However, most of these roses are noted for their richly scented flowers with a multitude of petals – often "quartered" or folded into tightly packed sections – in a range of colours from the palest to the deepest pink and including mauves, purples, maroon and white. The Gallicas are the smallest of the once-flowering group, suitable for most gardens. The Damasks are laxer, as are the Centifolias (the original Cabbage roses), their sumptuous double blooms bowed down right to the ground unless some support is given. The same could be said of the Moss roses, but most of the Albas will make big, self-supporting shrubs with very attractive grey-green foliage.

The Bourbon roses, the Portlands and the Hybrid Perpetuals, as well as the China roses already mentioned, also count as old garden roses, but they are, to some extent at least, recurrent (i.e. repeat-flowering). The Bourbons and the Portlands were the first roses in the West to have this characteristic, as a result of the introduction of China rose genes into the bloodstream, for roses from the Far East had always been repeat-flowering. The Portland group are smaller and more manageable bushes than the very robust Bourbons, some of which grow so strongly that they can be used as short climbers. The tall and often leggy Hybrid Perpetuals had their heyday in the Victorian period, when they were sometimes pegged down – the canes bent over and the tips tied to pegs in the ground to induce flowering shoots along their entire length – which was very effective, if a lot of trouble. China roses make small to medium-sized bushes, light and airy in habit, and are probably the most continuously in flower of all.

MODERN SHRUB ROSES

These vary just as much as the old garden roses, though there are fewer distinct groups among them. The two main ones, both repeat-flowering, are the Rugosas, originally from Japan and China and including such favourites as wine-red 'Roseraie de l'Hay' and white 'Blanc Double de Coubert', and the Hybrid Musks, typified by 'Penelope' and 'Felicia'. Other modern shrub roses include the giant cluster-flowered (Floribunda) types like 'Fred Loads' and 'Dorothy Wheatcroft', and the low-growing, mound-forming roses such as 'Ballerina' and 'Pearl Drift', which are quite small and ideal where space is limited.

In general the term shrub rose is applied to species or wild roses and their close relatives and old garden roses, as well as to their modern successors. A shrub rose could, I suppose, be defined as any rose whose large size or habit of growth makes it unsuitable for bedding. Which brings us to the two main groups of bedding roses.

LARGE-FLOWERED ROSES (HYBRID TEAS)

These are descended from Hybrid Perpetuals crossed with Tea roses from China, the latter giving our modern roses their elegant, high-centred flower form. They are sturdy and generally upright shrubs of fairly uniform growth, carrying large flowers, either one to a stem or three or four, from midsummer into autumn. Heights

'Alexander' is an exceptionally tall large-flowered rose

range from the 2½ ft (76 cm) of 'Alpine Sunset' or 'Just Joey' to the 4–5 ft (1.2–1.5 m) of 'Peace', or even more with roses like 'Alexander', though the majority are between these two extremes. The leaves are large and often glossy.

CLUSTER-FLOWERED ROSES (FLORIBUNDAS)

Derived from the rambling, cluster-flowered species R. *multiflora* (R. *polyantha*) and a China rose, these are similar in size and habit of growth to the large-flowered roses. However, their flowers are smaller and are carried in clusters or trusses of up to 30 blooms, though the average is less than this. A tall variety* would be the 4 ft (1.2 m) 'Anne Harkness', with the 2 ft (60 cm) 'Bright Smile' at the other end of the range. Pink 'Queen Elizabeth', at 8 ft (2.4 m) plus, is exceptional – so tall, really, as to make it a shrub rose.

CLIMBING ROSES

Many of these are descended from extra-vigorous wild roses from the Far East, which have long canes bearing hooked prickles or

*The word "variety" should be understood as "cultivated variety" throughout.

Above: 'Anne Harkness', a cluster-flowered rose with large trusses
Below: 'Pink Bells', a small spreading shrub rose which gives good
ground cover

thorns to support them when they scramble up through other shrubs in the wild. In the garden, if climbing roses are trained on any other kind of support, they need the help of tying in. In other words they are not true climbers, neither twining as honeysuckle does nor self-clinging like ivy.

Climbing roses are divided into two groups, climbers and ramblers. The latter are once-flowering and in general have large heads of quite small – sometimes very small – flowers. Climbers have thicker, less flexible canes and carry comparatively large flowers in small clusters. Many of them, especially the modern varieties, are recurrent.

Occasionally a climber arises as a sport of a bush rose. This is a genetic change in an individual plant which results in exceptionally long shoots, so that it becomes a climber and can be propagated to produce further climbers. When the word "Climbing" or the abbreviation "Cl." appears before the variety name of a rose in a nursery catalogue, for example, 'Cl. Wendy Cussons', this should mean that it is a climbing sport. But some care is necessary when choosing such varieties. By no means all the climbing sports flower well a second time, however recurrent the bush form may be. Some produce no second crop of blooms at all, so this is an important point to check with your supplier.

GROUND-COVER ROSES

Many of these have been developed from the rambler R. wichuraiana and their long stems spread across the ground, rooting as they go, to form a mat of leaves which weeds, at least in theory, should find difficult to penetrate. Other ground-cover roses are simply low-growing, wide-spreading bushes, modern shrub roses such as 'Bonica' and 'Smarty', which will hamper the growth of weeds as well, though it will take both kinds some years before they become really effective.

MINIATURE ROSES

These are tiny versions of the large- and cluster-flowered roses. Once again they are descended from a Chinese original, R. chinensis 'Minima', which has pink flowers. Hybridization with cluster-flowered varieties has widened the colour range, bringing in yellow, orange and flame, but it has also resulted in larger blooms and bushes. The bigger of these in-between roses, half way between a miniature and a cluster-flowered rose, are now known officially as dwarf cluster-flowered roses and more popularly as patio roses.

11

Getting the best from roses

Many people think of roses purely in terms of bedding, allocating them their own separate bed in the garden, and of course they are excellent for the purpose, especially the large-flowered and cluster-flowered types. But apart from bedding, roses can be used to make the most colourful hedges of almost any height, for climbing on walls and fences, over arches, pergolas and screens and up trees, for hiding unsightly sheds and outbuildings, as ground cover, in shrub borders either alone or mixed with other shrubs, for edging and in tubs and troughs.

BEDDING

Roses for bedding can be in flower for fully six months of the year and come in a very wide range of colours. Cluster-flowered varieties will give more continuous bloom than the large-flowered kinds, though the latter will provide blooms of the highest quality in great abundance. Some of the China roses can be used for bedding too – varieties like soft pink 'Hermosa' – but not if you are after startling colours. They will make a bed of quiet distinction, as opposed to the cockatoo screech of an orange-scarlet cluster-flowered rose like 'Topsi', which will have its place, but not with the Chinas.

There is no reason why varieties should not be mixed in a bed, but remember that flowering times may differ slightly. A further consideration is the size of the bed and where it is situated. If it is against a wall, it may be a good idea to have short varieties in the front and much taller ones behind them. On the other hand, if it is a big bed perhaps set on its own in a lawn and you wish to mix your roses, it will be found more satisfactory to plant them in groups of five or six of each kind. In this case make sure that the different varieties are of more of less uniform height and that the colours of adjoining roses blend happily. White roses and those with soft colours, like creamy pink 'Camphill Glory' or creamy yellow 'Peaudouce', can be used to separate strong colours that might otherwise conflict.

A round rose bed would give a striking effect if perhaps five different-coloured roses were planted to radiate from the centre like the slices of a cake, and a standard rose could be placed in the middle to add height. Standards can also be used in a long bed bordering a path, planted at intervals of about 5–6 ft (1.5–1.8 m)

A species or wild rose such as 'Canary Bird' will fit into a small garden if grown as a standard; it flowers in late spring

with bedding roses below them, or they may be grown as individual specimens to make a distinctive feature.

Standard roses are usually bush varieties which have been budded or grafted to the top of a $3\frac{1}{2}$ ft (1.07 m) stem from a root-stock (see also p.31). Both large- and cluster-flowered varieties are available as standards, together with a number of the less rampant shrub roses. Weeping standards are ramblers which have been treated in the same way, and their supple canes hang down laden with blossom.

HEDGING

Roses make the most colourful hedges imaginable. However, unless you choose tall, upright cluster-flowered roses, like pinky orange 'Fragrant Delight' and yellow 'Mountbatten', which do not spread out too much, you must allow a good deal of space. Traditional hedging roses, such as the Rugosa 'Roseraie de l'Hay' and some of the Hybrid Musks like 'Penelope' and 'Felicia', will produce hedges of great beauty 5 ft (1.5 m) or more high, but they will be at least 4–5 ft (1.2–1.5 m) in width. The Hybrid Musks in particular are prone to send out strong branches at odd and often inconvenient angles, though they can quite easily be trained on a chain-link fence or along horizontal wires like a climber. This will

The modern climber 'Golden Showers' is deservedly popular and particularly useful in small gardens because of its short growth

reduce width to more manageable proportions, but will not affect the breathtaking show of bloom that they will put on at mid-summer and again in the autumn, provided a certain amount of deadheading is done.

WALLS, FENCES, ARCHES AND PERGOLAS

Roses will climb up, over or into practically anything. They will cover walls, fences and trelliswork, will form tall screens if trained on a framework of rustic poles and will clothe arches and pergolas. The shorter varieties can be used as pillar roses, trained on a single pillar or pole. Ramblers like 'Sander's White' and 'François Juranville' are easy to train over arches and other structures because of their very flexible canes. But remember that, though they may put on an almost unbelievable display of bloom during the summer, there will be no repeat later. Many of the modern climbers, such as pink 'Morning Jewel' and apricot-pink 'Compassion', will provide later flowers, so that if you have space for only one or two climbing roses, these will be a better choice.

One of the loveliest ways of growing climbers and ramblers is up trees, which will be discussed on p.34.

'Fragrant Delight', an excellent bedding rose and also suitable for hedges, with coppery leaves to set off the flowers

GROUND COVER

Some ground-cover roses could almost be described as climbers that do not climb. These are descended from the rambler R. wichuraiana which, when left to its own devices, will spread across the ground, rooting where its shoots touch, rather than clamber upwards. Pink 'Max Graf' (there are now white and red versions) is perhaps the best known of the Wichuraiana hybrids, and more modern ones are represented in the Gamebird series, 'Pheasant', 'Partridge' and 'Grouse', raised by the famous breeder, Kordes of Germany. They are useful for covering a difficult bank or tumbling in a cascade of blossom over a retaining wall, but they will spread out in time to 15 ft (4.5 m) or more, which is a great deal further than most people would want for conventional ground cover. I am not sure that in due course they would not cover a football pitch, so if space is a problem, it is better to choose one of the many low-growing, spreading shrub roses, such as 'Rosy Cushion', 'Bonica' and 'Ferdy', which will form dense mounds no more than 3–4 ft (1–1.2 m) across.

As with all ground cover, it is essential to start with weed-free soil and in particular to remove perennial weeds before planting (see also the Wisley handbook, Ground cover plants).

Above: the dark red Bourbon 'Gipsy Boy' ('Zigeunerknabe') scrambling through a large bush of *Rosa × dupontii*
Below: miniature roses massed in a raised bed at Regent's Park

SHRUB BORDERS

The majority of shrub roses will mix very happily with shrubs in a border, provided they have plenty of sun. Some that flower only at midsummer (as, of course, do many other shrubs) will produce decorative hips in the autumn, while others like the Rugosas and Albas have very attractive foliage – an asset to any shrub border even when the flowers have gone.

There are a few shrub roses that can best be called scramblers. These will clamber up, into and through any other shrub that happens to be near them, spangling, for instance, a rather dull holly with their clusters of bloom in the most enchanting way. Examples of this kind of rose are 'Complicata', with its huge pink, white-eyed flowers, and 'Scarlet Fire'.

A rose like R. × dupontii or R. glauca (R. rubrifolia) or one of the bigger modern shrub roses, such as 'Nevada' or its pink sport 'Marguerite Hilling', is excellent as a specimen plant in a lawn or as a focal point at the end of a broad grass walk. Shrub roses vary so enormously, both in size and in habit of growth, that their uses in the garden are almost limitless. The more vigorous ones, like the Moss rose 'William Lobb' and the Bourbon 'Mme Isaac Pereire', can even be grown as low climbers, while others,as we have seen, are suitable for hedging and ground cover.

RAISED BEDS, TROUGHS AND CONTAINERS

One can grow miniature roses in troughs, where they must be watered regularly, but they are probably best of all in raised, terraced beds, with or without brick retaining walls. In both cases the roses are lifted some way above ground level, where it is much easier to enjoy their exquisite little flowers.

Tubs and window boxes can also provide a home for miniature and patio roses, again remembering to water them often, and are useful where space is limited. In the garden they make the most attractive edging plants for paths and drives, giving colour over a long period. However, if they are used to edge beds of large- or cluster-flowered roses, they tend to be overwhelmed or shaded from the sun they love.

The fact that miniature roses are so often sold in pots in garden centres, stores and greengrocers has led to a common misconception that they are houseplants. In the dry air of a centrally heated house the leaves would soon yellow and drop off. You can keep them in their pots in a cold greenhouse or out of doors and bring them into the house when the buds are showing colour, taking them out again when flowering is over.

Roses are happy with other plants

That roses have to be grown on their own is one of the many myths connected with rose-growing. However, it is probably true to say that the large-flowered and cluster-flowered varieties, with their rather stiff, upright stance, do not mix with other plants as happily as the other kinds, the old and modern shrub roses and the climbers and ramblers.

Climbing roses can be greatly enhanced, particularly if they flower only once or there is a long midsummer gap between flushes, by growing them up through another wall shrub. *Chaenomeles* and *Forsythia suspensa* will both flower before the roses, *Ceanothus* will flower with them and look delightful with white varieties. Alternatively, you can let one of the August/September-flowering clematis grow up through them. Avoid clematis species or run the risk of having your rose strangled. Choose instead one of the large-flowered hybrids that need yearly cutting down to a foot or so (30 cm) above the ground, and it and the rose will be the most happy of companions. A blue clematis such as 'Perle d'Azur' and a white rose like 'Climbing Iceberg' or 'White Cockade' look wonderful together.

Whether one should underplant bedding roses is a matter for debate. On the one hand underplanting will make mulching difficult if not impossible, the application of fertilizers tricky and operations like spraying, if the bed is wide, fraught with problems. Gardening has enough headaches already without adding to them, and in any case bedding roses should be planted close enough together for little if any soil to show.

There is, however, another side to the argument, for there are long periods in the winter months and in spring just after the roses have been pruned, when the beds will be anything but beautiful. Then winter-flowering pansies or violas make unbeatable cover and it does not matter too much if the roses tend to overwhelm them later on. Their seedlings can always be moved to act as edging.

Though by no means essential, the right edging round a rose bed can enhance it like a frame for a picture. Grey-leaved plants always look well, and a number of these supply in their flowers the blue lacking in the spectrum of rose colours. *Anaphalis cinnamomea* or *A. triplinervis*, *Pterocephalus perennis* (*P. parnassi*, *Scabiosa pterocephala*), which has tiny, pink, scabious-like blooms, dwarf shrubs such as the common or garden sage, *Salvia officinalis*,

Above: *Forsythia suspensa* on a house wall, flowering in early spring
and hiding the bare stems of climbing roses
Below: the same wall in late June, when the roses are in full bloom –
from front to back 'Danse du Feu', 'Elegance' and 'Aloha'

one of the smaller lavenders like *Lavandula* 'Munstead', a geranium such as 'Johnson's Blue' or the much smaller, white-eyed 'Buxton's Variety' are all possibilities. So too are the violet-blue *Campanula carpatica* 'Jewel' and catmint, *Napeta × faasenii*, if it can be kept from sprawling too much.

For growing among shrub roses, which tend to have lax, arching branches, there is nothing like the complete contrast given by the tall spires of lilies, provided that you have the kind of soil in which they thrive. If you are growing modern shrub roses, which include yellow, oranges and vermilions, you can incorporate lilies in that colour range, though white will also look good. With the old roses, however, white lilies such as that old favourite *Lilium regale* and many of the pink ones are best and the stronger, clashing colours should be avoided. Foxgloves also give the right effect and, since they seed themselves freely (too much so at times), they will never have to be renewed.

Otherwise shrub roses can be interplanted with the taller-growing, cream-flowered, grey-leaved potentillas like *P.* 'Vilmoriniana', rosemary, *Rosmarinus officinalis*, *Senecio* 'Sunshine' (as long as the yellow flowers are removed at the bud stage) or any of the various forms of *Santolina*. There are, in fact, hundreds of plants that will blend with roses very happily. There is nothing like experimenting to come up with the most unlikely but nevertheless beautiful combinations. Purple- and pink- leaved plants would, I feel, be worth a trial, though I have never used them myself.

Plants with grey foliage and blue or mauve flowers set off roses particularly well

Choosing and buying roses

Roses are sold in two main forms – bare-root and container-grown. Bare-root plants have been grown in the nursery fields and are then lifted during the dormant season for selling. This is still the traditional way to buy roses. However, increasing numbers of bare-root roses are pre-packed and sold through stores and supermarkets. If you really know what you are looking for, it is possible to get excellent plants, but beware of those with wrinkled, dried-up stems or premature growth caused by the greenhouse atmosphere of the packet. The hot atmosphere of the shop itself is rarely ideal and it is sensible to buy within a few days of the roses appearing on the shelves.

Beware, too, of specimens with spindly little shoots, sometimes discoloured with disease. There is a British Standard for roses and wherever you buy them from they should conform to it, for it is a minimum standard. It says, in effect, that large-flowered, cluster-flowered and shrub roses should have a good, fibrous root system and a minimum of two strong, firm shoots, no thinner than a pencil but preferably thicker. Standard roses should be double-budded, that is, with two points of origin for the shoots at the top of the stem.

Very popular nowadays are the container-grown roses on sale at every garden centre, which can be planted not only in winter but right through the summer months. However, do not be beguiled by a pretty spray of flowers, which may take your attention away from a poor plant underneath. And try to make sure that the roses are genuine container plants, not bare-root plants from the previous autumn, which have been crammed into containers to get rid of them. You can tell that the roses have been in their containers for the proper length of time by moss or algae on the soil surface, or roots beginning to push through the holes in the base of the container, and you can always ask. If you go to a reliable nursery, there should be no problems.

Many people are quite happy to choose their roses from a catalogue, even if the colour reproduction may be somewhat misleading. The disadvantage of this method is that you do not always learn the whole story about a particular variety – whether, for instance, it will fade in strong sun (though the catalogue will say if it does not), whether it withstands rain, whether it drops its petals cleanly after flowering or, indeed, whether it is exceptionally prone to disease. There is a reason for this latter

A model garden at the gardens of The Royal National Rose Society near St Albans

omission, in that a rose may be quite healthy in one part of the country but not in another.

There is no doubt at all that the best way to choose roses is to see them growing in garden conditions, if possible over a full season in your own area and in soil of the same type as in your garden. You will then be able to judge any defects, as well as knowing just what size of rose you are getting and how far apart to plant it. This is not something you can tell from seeing immature specimens in the nursery fields or in containers.

The Royal Horticultural Society's Garden, Wisley, the gardens of The Royal National Rose Society near St Albans, Queen Mary's Garden in Regent's Park, London, are famous examples of gardens where a wide range of roses is grown, all clearly labelled. Some rose nurseries also have display gardens. These are the places to go to decide what you want and maybe to discover undreamed-of delights. And when you have made your choice, go to a reputable nursery for your plants (see also p.62 for a list of gardens and nurseries).

The best of sites

SITUATION AND SOIL

Roses revel in the sun and will only do really well if they have it for most of the day. They like soil that retains moisture but at the same time is well drained, which may sound something of a contradiction, though many soils do achieve this – or can be helped to do so. Contrary to popular belief, they do not prefer clay, but they will be content in clay soil of the kind that drains well because, by its nature, it will retain a good deal of moisture. If on the other hand it is so heavy that it prevents moisture draining away, the roses will languish and die. They are not bog plants.

Roses tolerate both acid and alkaline soils, the ideal being a slightly acid soil (pH 6.5).

It is regrettable but true that old rose beds should not be replanted with new roses. After a few years the soil will have become "rose sick", a condition about which there is still considerable debate. Whatever its cause (the latest thinking is that a minute fungus attacks the tiny feeding roots of new roses, but finds the tough old roots of mature plants indigestible), the roses will not do well, and the easiest solution, provided that you have room, is to choose another situation for your rose bed. Otherwise it means either changing the soil in the bed completely – a labour of Hercules – or else sterilizing it, which can be a messy and tedious job. However, if you want to replace only a few roses in an established bed, the situation is more manageable. All that is required is to take out soil to a depth of about 18 in. (45 cm) for each rose, making the holes about 2 ft (60 cm) across, and to add fresh soil when planting. The soil removed can safely be disposed of in another part of the garden.

PREPARATION

When you are creating a completely new rose bed, it should not be necessary, unless your soil is exceptionally heavy and badly drained, to carry out double digging. Some digging, yes, for your roses will be in their new home for a long time and it is only sensible to give them the best send-off possible. While you are doing it – to about one spade's depth, breaking up the subsoil below this with a fork – remove any weeds and incorporate plenty of organic material, such as well-rotted stable manure (if you can get it) or compost, to improve the soil structure and provide plant foods. Peat will help to improve water retention, but contains no nutrients and is expensive. Where tests indicate that a heavy clay soil is deficient in lime, a dressing of hydrated lime will help to improve its structure. Calcium sulphate or gypsum is sometimes used for this purpose, at rates up to 2 lb per sq. yd (900 g per 0.84 m²), as it does not increase soil alkalinity.

All roses will benefit from this initial preparation of the soil. Do your digging well in advance of planting, to allow time for the organic matter which has been incorporated to break down in the soil. September is a good, though sometimes rather hot, month to carry out digging if you have planned for planting in the traditional – and best – month of November.

PLANTING DISTANCES

Planting distances depend of course on how big the plants will become. Among the large-flowered roses, for instance, a narrow, upright grower such as 'Grandpa Dickson' needs less space between bushes than a more spreading rose like 'Wendy Cussons'. In general, however, 1½–2 ft (45–60 cm) can be taken as an average distance for bedding roses.

Standard roses require at least 4 ft (1.2 m) between them and weeping standards even more. Shrub roses vary enormously in size, but vigorous ones should usually be spaced about 5 ft (1.5 m) apart or sufficient to allow room for development. When used for hedging, they can be planted more closely at 3–4 ft (1–1.2 m). Miniature roses should have about 1 ft (30 cm) between them.

PLANTING

Bare-root plants

November is the best month for planting, as the plants have time to settle in before the soil becomes too cold for root growth and will make a quicker start in the spring. But roses can be planted at any time when they are dormant or nearly so, which means from November to March, so long as you do not choose a frosty spell and the ground is not waterlogged. Autumn planting gets the job out of the way when there is probably not quite so much to do in the garden.

When you have unpacked your new roses, check them for damage and, if there are broken shoots, cut them away to the first healthy bud below the damage. At the same time shorten long, tough roots by about one half. Put the roses in a bucket of water to

Above: *Rosa foetida* 'Persiana', introduced in about 1838, became the main source of yellow in modern roses
Below: the modern shrub rose 'Ballerina' grown as a standard

soak or, if there are too many for this, dip them in water and wrap them in damp sacking. Prepare a planting mixture to give them a good start in life, about half a bucketful per rose made up of a 50/50 mixture of peat and garden soil, with a small handful of slow-release fertilizer such as bonemeal mixed well in. This can be taken to the planting site in a wheelbarrow.

The planting holes themselves should be deep enough for the budding union of the rose (i.e. the point where the plant is budded on to the rootstock, see p.31) to be about 1 in. (2.5 cm) below soil level, and wide enough for the roots to fan out as evenly as

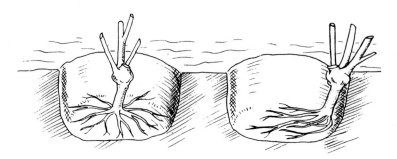

Figure 1:   two ways of planting a rose according to the natural direction of the roots

Figure 2:   planting a climber against a wall; the inset shows a vine eye driven into the brickwork to hold the supporting wires

possible all round, if they grow that way. Many roses have all their roots pointing in one direction (because of mechanical planting of rootstocks) and these should be placed at one side of the planting hole, not in the middle, and the roots then spread out as widely as you can (see figure 1). Hold the rose in position (it helps if you have three hands), tip the planting mixture over the roots and then fill up the hole with soil, treading firmly but not too hard, particularly if you have heavy soil that is likely to compact. Water well and re-firm the plants in the event of a hard frost the following winter or spring, which may have loosened them in the soil.

Planting to one side of the hole is again the answer with a climber against a wall, where the soil is often very dry. To get over this, dig the hole at least 18 in. (45 cm) away from the wall and direct the roots away from the base of the wall towards moister soil (see figure 2).

Standard roses need a relatively shallow hole, just enough for the roots to be covered. If they are more deeply planted, the root-stocks, which are usually Rugosa, will sucker freely. A standard is always supported with a stake, which should be driven into the hole before planting to avoid damaging the rose roots. The top of the stake should come up to the budding union, but no further.

Container-grown plants

Container-grown roses, as already stated, can be planted at any time. However, it is not simply a question of digging a hole of the same size as the root ball when it comes out of the container, pushing the plant in and leaving it to fend for itself. In heavy soils such a hole could form a sump from which water would be reluctant to drain and this, as we have seen, does not suit roses at all. So break up the surrounding soil and that at the base of the hole before you put the plant in, and use the planting mixture (see p.24) to fill in round the root ball. Take particular care that the rose finishes up at the right level in relation to the soil. Owing to the fact that containers are of standard size and the roots of roses are not, those with the biggest roots are likely to have the budding union well above the top of the soil in the container. This does not matter for a limited period, but in a permanent home the budding union should always be just below soil level to give it some protection from hard frosts. It is the most vulnerable part of the rose.

Keeping the roses going

Roses are such accommodating plants that they will keep growing and flowering – after a fashion – with very little attention. Nevertheless, if you really want to get the best out of them, there are jobs that should be done, not only to improve their immediate performance, but to help them to build up into strong plants for the future and hence to live longer. In addition, a robust, vigorous grower will be less seriously affected by disease.

FERTILIZERS

Mulches will be discussed below, and if you are using something like stable manure as a mulch this will provide a certain amount of plant food, though it is as well to supplement it. At one time keen rose growers used to mix up their own rose fertilizers, but there are now so many ready-mixed proprietary rose fertilizers on the market that it is really not worthwhile. They contain all a rose needs, including those constituents which are present in such small quantities that they are called trace elements, and which would be unlikely to be present in a home-made mixture.

A slow-release fertilizer such as bonemeal should be used when planting (see p.26) and subsequently all that is required is a small handful of a proprietary rose fertilizer sprinkled round the rose each year after pruning and lightly hoed in. Repeat this towards the end of July, but no later; otherwise sappy shoots would grow which would not be ripe enough to survive the frosts of winter.

MULCHING

Well-rotted stable manure, well-rotted compost, peat and shredded bark all make good mulches, the latter two improving the soil structure when they eventually break down, though not providing any plant foods. Mulching consists of spreading a layer about 3 in. (8 cm) thick of any of these materials over the surface of the soil, taking care, particularly with manure, that it does not come in direct contact with the rose stems. The mulch will serve a number of purposes: it will help to retain moisture in the soil (which means that you do not mulch in the middle of a drought unless you have watered artificially); it will suppress weeds (as long as the strong-growing perennial ones have been removed first); it will help maintain an even soil temperature; and, in the case of

Above: a delightful mixture of old roses – from left to right, 'Mme Hardy', 'Charles de Mills', 'Félicité Parmentier', *Rosa gallica* 'Versicolor' and the tall 'Pink Grootendorst'

Below: 'Iceberg' (left), an outstanding cluster-flowered rose which smothers itself in bloom from head to foot; the modern climber 'Bantry Bay' (right) can be trained up a pillar

manure and compost, it will supply some plant food as it breaks down. Mulches should go on in April when the soil has started to warm up slightly.

DEADHEADING

It is natural for a rose to produce hips after flowering, for these are the seed pods from which in due course seeds would come to begin a new generation. But with the production of seed pods, the rose has carried out its function for the year and, though it may produce some more flowers, there will be nothing to compare with the first flush. This is certainly not what we want with repeat-flowering roses. So the hips must be removed when the first blooming is over and the rose will start all over again. Deadheading is really a mini-pruning, and consists of cutting back the shoots that have borne flowers to a strong bud 4–5 in. (10–13 cm) down the stem. Roses grown especially for their decorative hips should not, of course, be deadheaded.

DISBUDDING

Disbudding is usually only necessary with large-flowered varieties, if you wish to obtain especially large blooms, perhaps for exhibition purposes or cutting. It can be very effective with a rose like 'Silver Jubilee'. In many cases the blooms are carried in a small cluster of three or four, particularly later in the season, and disbudding is a matter of removing all but the main central bud, which will then develop without competition from the others. In a few large-flowered roses – 'Pink Favourite' is one – the clusters of buds are so tightly packed that they do not have space to grow properly unless they are disbudded.

AUTUMN AND WINTER TASKS

Remove fallen leaves from around the roses and keep them clear of weeds, for both could harbour pests or their eggs. One school of thought advocates spraying the bare rose canes and the surrounding soil in winter with bordeaux mixture or a winter wash, in the belief that it will help to eradicate overwintering black spot spores. There is a conflict of evidence as to whether this works, and trials at Wisley have indicated that, if a spray is strong enough to be effective, it will also damage the plant tissue. However, if used at the manufacturer's recommended strength, a winter spray will certainly get rid of a number of undesirable pests and their eggs, if nothing else.

The shoots of tall-growing roses should be shortened by about

The large-flowered rose 'Silver Jubilee' produces even bigger blooms with disbudding

one half in late October or early November, to prevent the bushes being rocked by the winter winds and perhaps loosened in the soil. There is also a risk, particularly on clay soils, that a hollow in the soil may form at the base of the plant; this can fill with water, which may then freeze and damage the budding union when it thaws. An autumn pruning will help to avoid this problem.

DEALING WITH SUCKERS

The budding union of a rose, as already mentioned, is the point where it is budded onto a rootstock, and most of the roses available today are grown in this way rather than on their own roots. Different wild roses are chosen as rootstocks, their main purpose being to give a cultivated rose greater vigour. One of the commonest rootstocks is the dog rose, *Rosa canina*, and especially the selection 'Laxa', which is now widely used because it has much less tendency to sucker.

Shoots arising directly from the rootstock are suckers and, if they are not restrained, they will eventually swamp the less vigorous cultivated variety. Suckers must therefore be removed at the earliest possible moment and should be pulled off rather than

31

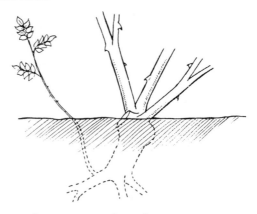

Figure 3: how a sucker grows out from the roots

cut. Pulling will remove dormant buds around the base of the sucker, while cutting would actually achieve the opposite of what is intended, leading to stronger growth from the sucker. Cutting is permissible only if a sucker is coming from right under a rose, when pulling might lift the plant bodily from the ground.

A beginner to rose-growing may have problems identifying a sucker. Many suckers have seven leaflets to a leaf as opposed to a cultivated variety's five, and this can be a useful first indication of a suspected sucker from a bedding rose. Remember, though, that cultivated varieties may occasionally have seven leaflets and a species will almost always do so. However, if the colour of the shoot and leaves – probably a lighter green – and colour and formation of the thorns are different, you are pretty certain to have a sucker on your hands. To make absolutely sure, find the point on the rose from which the sucker is growing, scraping away a little soil as required. If the shoot is growing from the roots below the budding union, it will be a sucker and should be removed (see figure 3).

Discipline in the rose garden

The purpose of training climbers and ramblers, which is what this chapter is about, is to achieve the maximum display of flowers. If the rose is left to its own devices, it will grow upward but not outwards and most of the flowers will appear at the top. If on the other hand the main canes are fanned out from the base and trained as near to the horizontal as possible, flowering shoots will be produced at the sides and the flowers will be borne all over the plant.

WALLS AND FENCES

On a fence or wall, a climbing rose should be trained along horizontal galvanized iron wires strung tightly between 4–5 in. (10–13 cm) vine eyes, which are driven into the woodwork, or into the mortar between the bricks (see figure 2, p.26, and figure 4, p.34). If the latter proves difficult, make a preliminary hole for each vine eye with a 3/16th in. (5 mm) drill. The vine eyes should be driven in so that the wires will be about 3 in. (8 cm) from the wall, and the rose canes may be secured to the wires with plastic ties.

Problems can arise when windows are rather close together, leaving not much wall space, particularly if they are the tall, Georgian type. There is little you can do about fanning the roses out sideways, and the best alternative is to choose some of the shorter-growing pillar roses such as 'Golden Showers' and 'Morning Jewel', which can be treated like tall wall shrubs and do tend to produce more flowers than most low down.

ARCHES, PERGOLAS, CATENARIES AND PILLARS

There is no doubt about it that the best roses for training over arches, pergolas and on catenary ropes (i.e. ropes slung between upright posts) are the ramblers, for their canes are far more flexible than those of climbers and hence more amenable to being directed where you wish them to go. They will make a spectacular display, but unfortunately only for about six weeks at midsummer or slightly later. For some people that is enough, but others want later flowers, in which case the alternative is to use recurrent climbers. Though their canes will be stiffer and less manageable, there should not be too many problems if training starts early when the shoots will be more pliable.

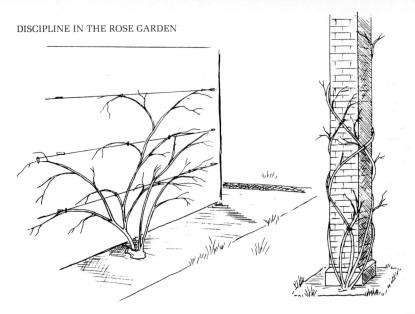

Figure 4: (left) training a climbing rose on horizontal wires against a wall; (right) training a climber or rambler in a spiral round the pillar of a pergola

Both pergolas and catenaries are supported by pillars, up which the roses have to grow first. Here once more the shoots cannot be fanned out horizontally, but they can be spiralled round the uprights to produce much the same effect (see figure 4). This method can be used for pillar roses as well.

If your climbers make rather slow progress at first, do not despair. It is usual for them to take two to three years to settle down before they really start to grow.

TREES

One of the loveliest and most exciting ways of growing climbers is up trees. The sight of waterfalls of white or soft pink blossom cascading from the branches of an otherwise dull old tree for weeks on end is one of those sensual delights that only gardening can produce, but a few warnings are necessary if one is to avoid setting up the ingredients for a potential disaster. A reasonably strong-growing rambler such as 'New Dawn' or 'Albéric Barbier' can safely be used to grow up an old apple tree or other tree of similar size. However, 'Kiftsgate', 'Wedding Day', 'Bobbie James'

Opposite: 'Morning Jewel' is an excellent modern climber where space is restricted

34

Ramblers like 'Félicite Perpétue' are ideal for growing over arches

and others of their kind, sold specifically nowadays as tree climbers, might easily bring any but the strongest of trees crashing to the ground in the gales of autumn. Untangling the results is not something to be contemplated lightly and, while I have no wish to be alarmist, make certain that your supporting tree is up to the job.

When the shoots of a rose are finding their way up through the branches, they will be seeking the sunshine, which will come from east, south and west. This means that you should not grow a rose up a tree on the southern boundary of your garden, for if you do, only your neighbours will benefit. Plant the rose anything up to 3–4 ft (1–1.2 m) away from the trunk of the tree, so that it is not robbed of too much light and does not have so much competition for food and water from the tree roots. Train it in towards the trunk along a strong cane or pole and, as it develops, tie it in to some of the lower branches of the tree. Before long the rose will begin to make its own way upwards without further help, particularly if it has been planted on the windward side of the tree, where the shoots will tend to be blown into the tree rather than away from it.

Pruning

Of all gardening jobs, pruning seems to inspire the greatest sense of unease in rose growers. Perhaps this is because the reasons for pruning are not always made clear, which makes it much more difficult to understand how to do it. So let us look at the basic principles.

A wild rose growing in the hedgerow demonstrates them very well. It sends up strong new shoots every year, and it is these that bear the best flowers. The following year they will have begun to deteriorate and will flower a little less profusely, but new shoots will have grown up. This process of replacement continues year by year and all we are doing when we prune is speeding it up, cutting away the wood that has flowered and encouraging the strong new shoots to come more quickly to produce the best blooms. At the same time we take the opportunity to remove dead and diseased wood and thin, weak shoots – those much less than pencil thickness, which will never carry good flowers – and we aim to achieve a balanced framework because it looks better than a lop-sided one. Lastly we open up the centre of the plant if it needs it, to admit more air and light and to get rid of any branches that may be crossing and rubbing together. All, when you come to think about it, pretty straightforward.

The question as to when you should prune is one to which different people give different answers. Some say prune in the autumn and some say prune in the spring, the truth of the matter being that both are right. Any time during or between these periods is suitable, for these are the months when roses are dormant or semi-dormant. The recommended pruning months are March in the south of the United Kingdom and April in the north, and both are fine. November pruning can be perfectly satisfactory, except perhaps when a very hard winter follows. Then it may be necessary to return to frost-damaged plants in the spring, cutting out wood that has died back. Never prune during a frosty spell, as newly cut wood will be particularly vulnerable.

How hard you prune depends to a certain extent on the type of rose, and these differences will be explained below (p.38). Very hard pruning is generally restricted to roses grown for exhibition, as it will produce bigger blooms, if fewer of them, which is not what is wanted for garden display. Roses should also be very hard pruned when they are newly planted, which involves taking your courage in both hands and cutting them back to 2–3 in. (5–8 cm) above ground level. It may seem a massacre, but they will benefit in the long run, gaining time to build up a good root system before having to divert energy to flowering shoots.

Another time for ruthlessness is when you take over an established garden in which there are old and neglected roses with gnarled, woody stumps and branches and a scarcity of new shoots. Unlikely as it may appear, many of these roses can be rejuvenated, for there will be long-dormant buds hidden away somewhere in the tough old bark. Cut back almost to ground level at pruning time, feed them well, and see what happens, If they do not survive this drastic treatment, they would probably not have survived for long anyway, but there is every chance they will take on a new lease of life. It is certainly worth trying.

In all pruning, make the cuts about $\frac{1}{4}$ in. (6.4 mm) above a leaf-axil bud, the cut sloping down away from the bud on the far side of the shoot (see figure 5). Choose an outward-facing bud if that is the way you want the new shoot to develop. With roses that sprawl, it may be better to select a bud facing inwards or even upwards to help fill in the centre of the bush. If when pruning you find that the centre of the stem is brown, it means that die-back is spreading down the shoot (see p.59). Cut again to the next bud and the next if necessary until white wood is reached, even if it involves going almost to the budding union.

So much for generalities. Now for the roses.

PRUNING DIFFERENT TYPES OF ROSES

Large-flowered varieties

Carry out a general clearance of dead, diseased and spindly wood as outlined above and then reduce the main shoots to about 8 in. (20 cm). Do not take a ruler to it: cut to the nearest bud (see figure 6).

Cluster-flowered varieties

Prune as for large-flowered roses but less severely, since the size and quality of individual blooms is not so crucial. Reduce the main shoots to about 10–12 in. (25–30 cm; see figure 7).

Climbers

These form a permanent framework of main canes and normally only the side shoots need attention, cutting them back by about two thirds in autumn (see figure 8). However, if the rose is getting

Figure 5: the correct pruning cut just above a bud

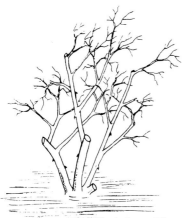

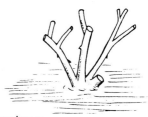

Figure 6: pruning a large-flowered rose

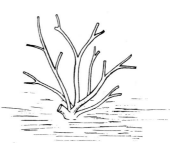

Figure 7: pruning a cluster-flowered rose

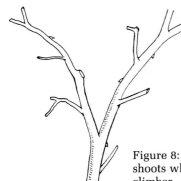

Figure 8: shortening the side shoots when pruning a climber

out of hand, you can shorten a main shoot. If it is becoming very leggy, prune one or two main shoots, cutting them back really hard to encourage branching near the base.

Ramblers

If these are not dealt with each year, they can get into a fine old tangle, but many people who grow them do not particularly mind this and regard it as one of their charms – or so they say, for sorting out a rambler when pruning it can be a daunting task. However, if perfection is the aim, prune when they have finished flowering in late summer: the shoots that have carried flowers are cut right to the base and the strong new shoots that should have grown up from ground level are tied in to replace them. If there are not enough new shoots, keep some of the old ones, tipping them and reducing the side shoots. They will still bear some flowers the following summer.

Shrub roses

It is difficult to give any general instructions for pruning these as they are so diverse. In my experience the species roses lose their charm if they are pruned, except for the removal of dead or decayed wood. Most other shrub roses, however, flower more freely if the main and side shoots are shortened by about one third in winter. They will make tidier bushes too. Those modern shrub roses that are, in fact, giant cluster-flowered varieties, like 'Fred Loads' and 'Chinatown', should be reduced in height by about one third.

In general, shrub roses used for hedges are pruned as if they were individual bushes. However, Rugosas and Gallicas can be clipped over gently with shears. Follow their natural outline and do not attempt formal shaping as for a beech or privet hedge.

Miniature roses

These can be treated as tiny cluster-flowered varieties and their height reduced by about one third after the removal of dead and diseased wood. Some thinning may be needed with the very twiggy kinds to allow air to circulate.

And now for the roses

The following roses have been chosen because I know from growing them myself that they are good varieties; a large number of them have, in addition, won awards in The Royal National Rose Society's trials. The name of the raiser and date of introduction is given in brackets after the name of each rose, together with any alternative name. All heights should be taken as indications only, since soil, growing conditions and many other factors cause great variation in the same variety of rose.

LARGE-FLOWERED ROSES (HYBRID TEAS)

In the descriptions of the large-flowered and cluster-flowered roses, short means 2 ft (60 cm) and under, medium means 2–3 ft (60 cm–1 m), and tall means over 3 ft (1 m).

'**Alec's Red**' (Cocker, 1970) Strongly scented, cherry-red, very double and rather globular blooms, freely carried on a strong, bushy plant of medium height. (See p.42.)

'**Alexander**' (Harkness, 1972) A very tall grower, up to 6 ft (1.1 m) and suitable for hedges. Healthy, dark green leaves and moderately full, deep vermilion blooms only slightly scented. (See p.9.)

'**Blessings**' (Gregory, 1968) By no means a newcomer, but still one of the best in its colour range for freedom of flowering. Blooms large, opening rather loosely, salmon pink. Slight scent. A fine, vigorous grower. Medium to tall.

'**Cheshire Life**' (Fryer, 1972) Fairly large and moderately full, deep vermilion blooms freely borne on a well-branched plant of medium height.

'**Congratulations**' (Kordes, 1978) A first-rate rose only gradually making its name. Tall and upright, it will reach about 5 ft (1.5 m). The medium-sized, soft rose-pink blooms will last for ages in water and have long, thornless stems. Healthy, medium green leaves.

'**Doris Tysterman**' (Wisbech Plant Co, 1975) Moderately fragrant, quite full, orange-red blooms carried freely on a plant of medium height. The dark green foliage may be susceptible to mildew in a bad year.

'**Dutch Gold**' (Wisbech Plant Co, 1987) Vigorous and bushy with strong stems reaching medium height. The large, deep green foliage shows off well the very large, double yellow blooms which stand rain remarkably well for their size. Some fragrance. (See p.42.)

'**Elizabeth Harkness**' (Harkness, 1969) Ivory-white with a touch of pink describes the colour of these always immaculately shaped blooms, which first appear early in the season. The plant is bushy, of medium height, and the dark green leaves are healthy.

'**Fragrant Cloud**' (Tantau, 1963) Blooms with the freedom of a cluster-flowered rose, under which category it is grouped in its native Germany. Huge, double blooms in dusky geranium-red with the sweetest of scents and tremendous continuity. The bushy plant is well covered with leaves, but is not entirely proof against disease. (See p.42.)

Large-flowered roses – 'Alec's Red' (left), 'Dutch Gold' (right)

'**Freedom**' (Dickson, 1983) This Gold Medal winner is one of the best bright yellow roses of recent years. Of medium height, the plant is bushy and carries moderately scented, fairly full flowers freely throughout the summer.

'**Just Joey**' (Cant, 1973) One of the truly great roses and excellent for bedding. Of medium height and well covered with healthy deep green foliage, the plant bears the most enchanting, very large blooms with waved and frilled petals in a soft coppery pink. Only moderate scent.

'**Keepsake**' (Kordes, 1981) Very large and shapely, rosy carmine blooms, often of exhibition standard, and in a colour not found in many other roses. A strong bush of medium height, it has fine, leathery, healthy leaves. Could, perhaps, be more generous with its flowering, but each flush is worth waiting for.

'**Lovers' Meeting**' (Gandy, 1980) The bronze-green leaves of this bushy, upright plant of medium height set off to perfection the beautifully shaped, fairly large, bright orange flowers. A strong, healthy grower, not always a characteristic of roses in this colour. Sometimes classed as a cluster-flowered variety.

'**National Trust**' (McGredy, 1970) A short to medium grower, this makes the ideal bedding rose, its bright red blooms freely carried and always immaculate in shape. Its record for health is sound.

'**Paul Shirville**' (Harkness, 1983) Originally classified as a cluster-flowered variety because of the freedom with which it bears its clusters of peachy pink, double blooms. However, their size indicated that it was really a large-flowered rose. Not that this makes a scrap of difference to its beauty, its fine, healthy foliage and the bushy, vigorous growth to medium height. Outstanding. Fragrant. (See p.2.)

'Fragrant Cloud' (left), 'Keepsake' (right)

'Lovers' Meeting' (left), 'Precious Platinum' (right)

'Peace' (Meilland, 1942) A classic. Huge, pale yellow double blooms with attractively waved petals on an equally large bush that can be used for hedging. Healthy, leathery leaves, but a tendency to produce blind shoots early in the season.

'Peaudouce' (Dickson, 1985) A tall grower carrying on its long, strong stems with great abundance very large, elegant, creamy primrose blooms of exhibition quality. Unlike most show blooms, they stand rain well. The leaves are rich dark green and very healthy. Some fragrance. Superb for a large bed and for cutting for the house.

'Piccadilly' (McGredy, 1959) A red and yellow bicolour about thirty years old. The flowers are very freely carried and quick to repeat, shapely but with little scent. As they age, the red suffuses the yellow of the petal reverse. A bushy plant with glossy, deep green foliage. Prone to black spot.

'Pink Favourite' (Von Abrams, 1956) The large glossy foliage is exceptionally healthy on this vigorous, upright plant of medium height. Large, bright rose-pink blooms of exhibition standard if disbudded.

'Polar Star' (Tantau, 1982) Looks like being the white large-flowered rose we have all been waiting for, rainproof (or as rainproof as any rose is) and healthy. Its beautifully shaped blooms are carried on a strong plant of medium height and with good, dark foliage.

'Pot o' Gold' (Dickson, 1980) A very sound, yellow bedding rose of medium height with fairly large, full blooms borne in profusion.

'Precious Platinum' (Dickson, 1974) The large, shapely blooms are bright red (despite the name) and come with a freedom that makes this rose, when combined with its bushy growth to medium height, a fine choice for bedding.

'Rosemary Harkness' (Harkness, 1985) A bushy plant, medium to tall, carrying fairly large, double blooms in orange-salmon with an orange-yellow reverse. Fine scent.

'Royal William' (Kordes, 1984) Large, double, deep red blooms with a good scent on a medium-sized, upright plant with healthy foliage.

'Silver Jubilee' (Cocker, 1978) Provides a practically non-stop display of its shapely, peach-pink, slightly fragrant flowers on a bushy and very thorny plant, which has fine, glossy leaves with a good health record. With disbudding, blooms can be of exhibition standard. Outstanding in every way. (See p.31.)

'Solitaire' (McGredy, 1987) Large, very full, scented blooms in yellow edged with red, on a tall, very vigorous bush with fine, healthy, dark green leaves.

'The Lady' (Fryer, 1985) The blooms are large and full, yellow edged salmon-pink, a most pleasing combination. Upright growth to medium height and healthy.

'Troika' ('Royal Dane'; Poulsen, 1972) Large, moderately full blooms in orange-red shading to orange-pink and always striking. A medium to tall grower whose vigour and health make it excellent for bedding. Not much scent.

'**Whisky Mac**' (Tantau, 1967) A controversial choice – everybody's favourite for its soft, amber-yellow colouring and wonderful scent and yet with one of the poorest health records of any rose. Despite susceptibility to dieback, mildew and black spot, it sells and sells. Growth upright to medium height.

CLUSTER-FLOWERED ROSES (FLORIBUNDAS)

'**Amber Queen**' (Harkness, 1984) Quite low-growing but with large clusters of amber-yellow blooms, double, opening flat and with some scent. A good, bushy grower and first-rate bedding rose.

'**Anne Harkness**' (Harkness, 1980) A tall grower with huge clusters of apricot-orange flowers that do not appear until well into July and, with their long, strong stems, are ideal for cutting. A favourite with exhibitors, which means that the blooms last well. A very good health record. (See p.10.)

'**Arthur Bell**' (McGredy, 1965) Quite an old rose but one that seems to be ageless and has not been bettered as a strongly scented, tall, yellow bedding rose with fine healthy foliage. The yellow fades in strong sun, though not unattractively.

'**Avocet**' (Harkness, 1984) Large trusses of orange flowers edged coppery pink, scented and semi-double. The plant is of medium height and has dark green leaves.

'**Bright Smile**' (Dickson, 1980) A real charmer, a bushy, short grower in the patio rose mould. The flowers, which are semi-double, are quite large and carried in small trusses. Colour is the brightest, cleanest yellow. Health good.

'**Burma Star**' (Cocker, 1974) A tall grower which will make a good hedge, the clusters of light amber-yellow blooms being very showy. Can be a little uneven in growth, but in an informal hedge this does not matter.

'**Champagne Cocktail**' (Horner, 1985) The large trusses of pale yellow flowers are attractively flecked and splashed carmine, rather in the manner of the McGredy "hand-painted" varieties. Free flowering, of medium height, bushy and healthy.

'**City of Belfast**' (McGredy, 1968) Trusses of quite small, moderately full, scarlet blooms make this a stunning bedding rose. Height medium or less.

'**City of Leeds**' (McGredy, 1966) Of medium height, this is a fine bushy plant with moderately large clusters of semi-double, salmon-pink flowers that open flat and are relatively big. No scent but lasts well when cut. An excellent bedding rose, also useful for exhibitors.

'**Escapade**' (Harkness, 1967) Large trusses of eye-catching blooms – rosy violet with a white eye and the occasional pure white flower. Medium to tall, it makes a well-branched bush with glossy, bright green leaves. Good scent.

'**Evelyn Fison**' ('Irish Wonder'; McGredy, 1962) For long the best of the bright red cluster-flowered varieties, keeping its colour in sun and rainproof too. The blooms are moderately full and carried on trusses of variable size. The plant would benefit from more and larger leaves. Black spot cannot be ruled out.

'**Eye Paint**' (McGredy, 1976) If lightly pruned, this can make a substantial hedging shrub, but it can be kept to size for bedding. The showy flowers are produced in enormous trusses, small and scarlet with a white centre and back of the petal. Scentless, but very striking. Watch for black spot on the dark green leaves.

'**Fragrant Delight**' (Wisbech Plant Co, 1978) One of those roses whose worth has only slowly been recognized. Medium height with dark, coppery foliage which is a marvellous foil for the trusses of light orange-salmon, very fragrant flowers. (See p.15.)

Opposite: cluster-flowered roses – 'Amber Queen', 'Escapade' (top left and right); 'Eye Paint', 'Korresia' (centre left and right); 'Margaret Merril', 'Memento' (bottom left and right)

'**Glenfiddich**' (Cocker, 1976) A medium-sized, vigorous bush with trusses of amber-yellow, double flowers. Good for bedding and reputed to do better in the north.

'**Hannah Gordon**' (Kordes, 1983) Clusters of semi-double, quite large flowers in white, edged pink. Of medium height and bushy, this is an attractive bedding rose.

'**Iceberg**' (Kordes, 1958) One of the all-time great roses. A tall grower, it will make a shrub if lightly pruned, but is useful for bedding too. The white flowers are carried all over the plant, not just at the top. They have a delicate fragrance. Black spot on the rather pointed, glossy green leaves is said to be a problem. (See p.29.)

'**Invincible**' (De Ruiter, 1983) A very vigorous, medium to tall plant, with fine, very healthy, dark green, semi-glossy leaves. Carries medium-sized trusses of large double flowers in deep scarlet. They will shrug off the effects of sun or rain. Not too well known as yet, but clearly a rose with a future.

'**Korresia**' (Kordes, 1974) Of medium height, scented, profuse with its bloom and with good continuity, this is probably the finest of all the yellow bedding roses. Bushy growth and healthy foliage. (See p.45.)

'**Lilli Marlene**' (Kordes, 1959) A good rose still, after all this time, with its big trusses of dusky scarlet blooms, though it may need watching for disease. Growth bushy and height medium.

'**Liverpool Echo**' (McGredy, 1971) Large trusses of semi-double, fairly large blooms in soft salmon-pink make this a winner. The growth is strong, medium to tall, and well branched. Only slight scent.

'**Lovers' Meeting**' See p.42.

'**Margaret Merril**' (Harkness, 1978) The best white cluster-flowered rose since 'Iceberg', though very different in habit. The flowers are large, predominantly white but with a soft pink tinge in the centre, opening wide to show amber-pink stamens. With the bonus of a strong scent and fine dark foliage, it is a rose of note, even if prone to black spot. (See p.45.)

'**Matangi**' (McGredy, 1974) Bright orange-red blooms, the colour feathering in to a white centre in the manner of this raiser's other "hand-painted" varieties. Growth vigorous, medium to tall and well branched.

'**Memento**' (Dickson, 1978) One of the most constantly in flower of all bedding roses, bushy and of medium height, with large trusses of moderately full, bright salmon-orange blooms. It makes the most cheerful sight imaginable. (See p.45.)

'**News**' (Le Grice, 1968) Beetroot-purple is the raiser's description of the colour of the flowers, which does not really do the rose justice, though it is certainly unique. The blooms are large and carried on trusses of medium size. Growth bushy, height medium.

'**Princess Michael of Kent**' (Harkness, 1979) A fine yellow bedding rose with bright green, glossy foliage of exceptional health. The flowers are large, globular with many petals, and carried in trusses of five or six. Height medium.

'**Queen Elizabeth**' (Lammerts, 1955) A law unto itself, with a guardsman stance that will take it up to 8–9 ft (2.4–2.7 m). Often used for hedging, though most of the china-pink, cupped flowers will tend to be at the top. They have long, thornless stems, making them ideal for cutting and they last well in water. A very good health record.

'**Southampton**' (Harkness, 1972) Large clusters of apricot-orange blooms, sweetly scented and moderately full, repeating well and swiftly. A well branched plant with healthy mid-green leaves. Medium to tall and will make a good hedge.

'**Sue Lawley**' (McGredy, 1980) Carmine, pink and white, the colours feathering into one another, as this is a "hand-painted" rose. The flowers are large and carried in medium-sized trusses on a bushy plant with dark green leaves, growing to medium height. Scent only slight, but this is an interesting novelty.

'**The Times Rose**' (Kordes, 1984) Large clusters of very double, blood-red blooms borne above foliage of a dark, coppery red, giving a most striking effect. Growth

'Aloha' (left), a striking short climber or shrub with a long succession of bloom; the very prickly 'Maigold' (right) flowers in early summer, as the name suggests

very bushy and height medium. A wonderful bedding rose, seemingly disease-proof.

'Warrior' (Le Grice, 1978) A very short grower in the patio rose category, but one that makes its presence felt, for it has small trusses of double blooms of the most dazzling scarlet. Healthy but almost scentless.

CLIMBERS

'Aloha' (Boerner, 1949) A rose which has been slow to win recognition, but is now coming to the fore. Vigorous to about 10 ft (3 m). Large, very full flowers in rose-pink, sweetly scented and rainproof on long stems and excellent for cutting. Repeat-flowering. Healthy, bright green, glossy leaves. Also makes a good shrub.

'Bantry Bay' (McGredy, 1967) Of moderate vigour, reaching 10 ft (3 m) or so, it carries large clusters of medium-sized, semi-double pink blooms with great freedom. Good repeat. (See p.29.)

'Compassion' (Harkness, 1973) Elegant apricot-pink blooms with a sweet scent borne abundantly on a plant with glossy, deep green foliage. Fully recurrent. To 10 ft (3 m) or so.

'Dublin Bay' (McGredy, 1976) Large, bright crimson blooms in clusters of three or four, slightly scented and recurrent. Bushy up to about 8 ft (2.4 m) and rather slow to get going.

'Etoile de Hollande' (Leenders, 1931) Climbing form of the large-flowered bush rose of that name and an old favourite for its large, scented, deep dusky red blooms, loosely formed but produced in great numbers and a good repeat. To 12 ft (3.7 m) or more. Mildew possible.

'**Golden Showers**' (Lammerts, 1957) Tight, bright yellow buds opening to large, loosely formed flowers on long, thornless stems. Healthy, glossy foliage and a good repeat. To 8 ft (2.4 m). (See p.14.)

'**Handel**' (McGredy, 1965) Unique among climbers, the medium-sized, moderately full blooms open creamy white edged with cerise, which slowly spreads over the petals. Fully recurrent and reaching 12 ft (3.7 m) or so. Black spot a possibility.

'**Iceberg**' (Cant, 1968) A sport of the cluster-flowered bush rose (see p.46) and similar as to flowers and leaves. Recurrent and vigorous to 10 ft (3 m).

'**Maigold**' (Kordes, 1953) Flowering only in early summer, but what a show. Large, loosely formed, bronzy apricot flowers borne in profusion on a strong-growing, very thorny plant which will reach 10 ft (3 m). Shiny, dark green leaves. (See p.47.)

'**Morning Jewel**' (Cocker, 1968) Medium-sized clusters of moderately full, pink blooms carried in great abundance. Recurrent. Scent only slight. Vigorous to 10 ft (3 m). Good for a north wall. (See p.35.)

'**New Dawn**' (Int. Somerset, 1930) Recurrent sport of the rambler 'Dr W. Van Fleet', carrying large clusters of delightful pearly pink blooms with a sweet scent. Everybody's favourite. To 8–10 ft (2.4–3 m).

'**Pink Perpetue**' (Gregory, 1965) Large clusters of medium-sized blooms in carmine pink with a lighter reverse, borne with great freedom and with a good repeat in the autumn. Vigorous and bushy to 8 ft (2.4 m). One of the best.

RAMBLERS

'**Albéric Barbier**' (Barbier, 1900) The flowers are creamy white, opening from yellow buds and scented. Produced early in the summer only on a very vigorous grower to 15 ft (4.5 m). Almost evergreen with its fine, glossy foliage.

'**Albertine**' (Barbier, 1921) Despite the fact that it is prone to mildew and does not shed its petals cleanly when the flowers are over, this is still very popular for its sweetly scented, soft pink blooms carried in incredible profusion in early summer, set off by bronze-green leaves. Very vigorous up to 15 ft (4.5 m) and freely branching. (See p.63.)

'**Félicité Perpétue**' (Jacques, 1827) Huge clusters of white rosettes, each one crammed with petals and borne over a long period at midsummer. Fine dark foliage and prolific growth to 10 ft (3 m). (See p.36.)

'**François Juranville**' (Barbier, 1909) Thought by many to be the best of the Barbier ramblers. Clusters of numerous medium-sized blooms in salmon-pink over many weeks at midsummer. Only slight scent but plenty of vigour to 10 ft (3 m).

'**Phyllis Bide**' (Bide, 1923) A repeat-flowering rambler? A recurrent climber? No one is quite sure, but it is a rambler in habit with clusters of quite small flowers in a mixture of light yellow and pink, a lovely combination which continues almost non-stop throughout summer and autumn. Up to 12 ft (3.7 m). May be difficult to find, but specialists do stock it.

'**Seagull**' (Pritchard, 1907) Chosen to represent a large group of extremely free-flowering ramblers with huge heads of small, white, scented flowers. This one is less tall than some at about 12 ft (3.7 m), whereas 'Bobbie James' and 'Kiftsgate', for instance, can be used to climb tall trees.

SPECIES OR WILD ROSES

R. californica 'Plena' Semi-double form of an American species and one of the most free-flowering of all. The bright pink flowers with their prominent yellow stamens are carried on long, arching shoots on a bush which will get very big indeed, some 8–9 ft (2.4—2.7 m) tall and across. Fresh green, rather hairy leaves.

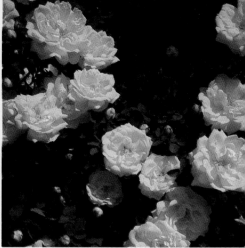

The vigorous *Rosa californica* 'Plena' (left) blooms in late June or July; the brilliant yellow flowers of *Rosa × harisonii* (right) have a rather strange, heavy scent

'Canary Bird' A shrub some 7 ft (2.1 m) high and wide with bright yellow flowers crowded along the arching shoots very early in the season. Scent good and foliage small and ferny, an attractive feature when the blooms have gone. Sometimes subject to die-back. (See p.13.)

R. × dupontii ('Dupontii') A most attractive rose bearing at midsummer a profusion of quite large, single flowers with very broad petals, blush-pink and fading to white. The sweet scent derives from Musk rose ancestry. It makes quite a large bush to 7 ft (2.1 m), fairly open-growing and with healthy, soft grey-green leaves. I have seen it used effectively as a short climber. (See p.16.)

R. foetida 'Persiana' ('Persian Yellow') Possibly a sport from *R. foetida* and a rose to grow not only because it is attractive in itself but because of its historical interest, being the parent of all our yellow bedding roses. A useful spreading bush some 5 ft (1.5 m) high or perhaps best as a short climber. Bright yellow, double flowers in midsummer, but look out for black spot on the glossy green leaves. (See p.25.)

R. glauca (*R. rubrifolia*) A species native to Europe grown mainly for its plum-purple new shoots and greyish purple leaves. The flowers are pink and fleeting, but result in bunches of bright red, round hips. To 8 by 7 ft (2.4 × 2.1 m). (See p.61.)

R. × harisonii ('Harison's Yellow') A very free-flowering yellow rose, often coming into bloom in late May. About 5 ft (1.5 cm) high, it is a shrub which will fit into quite a small garden, but is not the neatest of growers and may need trimming from time to time to keep it in shape. Healthy, bright green leaves.

R. moyesii 'Geranium' A seedling of *R. moyesii* raised at the RHS Garden, Wisley, and, being a little smaller than its parent, more suitable for a medium-sized plot. But only just, for it still makes an 8–9 ft (2.4–2.7 m), fairly open shrub, carrying at midsummer brilliant, single, crimson flowers with creamy stamens. These are followed by a fine show of bright orange-red, bottle-shaped hips which will last well into the autumn. Fairly small, rather rounded, dark green leaves.

R. × paulii 'Rosea' ('Paulii Rosea') The pink form of white *R. × paulii* and an exact duplicate in habit, perhaps marginally smaller. As a wide-spreading, low-growing bush, it is often recommended as a ground-cover rose, though it will reach 4 ft (1.2 m) or so in height. The incredibly thorny shoots carry large, single flowers of soft pink, surrounded by leafy bracts. The leaves are grey-green, showing off the richly scented blooms to perfection.

OLD GARDEN ROSES

These are once-flowering, unless otherwise stated.

'Celestial' ('Celeste') An Alba rose with the group's soft, grey-green foliage and blush-pink, semi-double blooms with a good fragrance. Bushy to 5–6 ft (1.5–1.8 m).

'Charles de Mills' ('Bizarre Triomphant') A Gallica rose making a generally upright, very twiggy bush of 5 ft (1.5 m) or so, with the rather rough-looking leaves of the group. The flowers, however, are of the utmost refinement, large and opening wide and flat, crammed with petals and often quartered. The colour is a deep crimson. Some scent. (See p.6.)

'Complicata' An unlikely-looking Gallica hybrid, making a big bush 5 ft (1.5 m) or more tall, happiest when its long shoots can scramble up through another shrub. The huge, saucer-like, single flowers are deep pink with a white eye and carried in tremendous profusion at midsummer.

'Comte de Chambord' A Portland rose, recurrent and with large, very double blooms in deep pink. Growth bushy up to 4 ft (1.2 m). Dates from 1860.

'Fantin Latour' Origin unknown but probably a Centifolia, even if it is more bushy and upright than most, making a large shrub. Midsummer-flowering with clusters of soft pink, very double blooms which have a good fragrance. (See p.63.)

'Königin von Dänemarck' An Alba raised in 1826. Grey-green foliage, clusters of quite small, but very double, pink flowers, with a deeper tone in the centre, and a moderate size make this an excellent old rose for the modern small garden.

'Mme Hardy' (Hardy, 1832) A Damask rose growing into a bush 6 by 5 ft (1.8 x 1.5 m) with bright green leaves and clusters of medium-sized, pure white flowers, opening wide to reveal a green "button" centre. Scent good.

'Old Blush' ('Parson's Pink China') One of the best of the China roses, making a bushy shrub up to 4 ft (1.2 m) tall, with a continuous display of loosely formed, pink flowers right up to Christmas. Introduced from China in about 1752.

R. gallica 'Versicolor' ('Rosa Mundi') The third Gallica in our list, a shrub similar to 'Charles de Mills', upright and twiggy. The flowers this time are loosely formed and only just double and have deep pink striping and splashes on a very pale pink to white ground. Makes a stunning hedge if you do not mind mildew later. Of seventeenth-century origin or perhaps even earlier.

MODERN SHRUB ROSES

'Ballerina' (Bentall, 1937) A low-growing, mounding shrub up to 4 ft (1.2 m), bearing huge heads of small flowers in pink and white, resembling apple blossom. Bright green, glossy leaves. Recurrent. (See p.25.)

'Constance Spry' (Austin, 1961) A modern rose crossed with the Gallica 'Belle Isis' has produced here a rose with great vigour and huge, cupped, very double blooms of rose pink with an attractive scent. The arching growth up to 6 ft (1.8 m) needs some support from a frame or wall. A beauty.

'Cornelia' (Pemberton, 1925) A Hybrid Musk with the usual bushy, rather unpredictable growth, ultimately reaching 5 ft (1.5 m) tall and across. Clusters of quite small, strawberry-pink, double flowers. Recurrent.

Opposite: the pink blooms of *Rosa × paulii* 'Rosea' (top) are particularly effective with their white centres and yellow stamens
Old garden roses – 'Complicata', 'Königin von Dänemarck' (centre left and right); 'Mme Hardy', *Rosa gallica* 'Versicolor' (bottom left and right)

'**Fred Loads**' (Holmes, 1967) A very tall cluster-flowered rose in habit, which will make an eye-catching 6 ft (1.8 m) hedge. Huge heads of large semi-double blooms in soft orange-vermilion and good, healthy foliage. Good for cutting and showing.

'**Fru Dagmar Hastrup**' ('Frau Dagmar Hartopp') The second name, though often used, is incorrect, as the rose was raised at the Hastrup nurseries in 1914. The most restrained of the Rugosa roses for a small garden, growing to only about 4 ft 1.2 m) and having the characteristic wrinkled Rugosa foliage. Large, single flowers, pale pink with creamy yellow stamens, followed by large, tomato-red hips from summer to autumn. Recurrent.

'**Frühlingsmorgen**' (Kordes, 1941) A bushy, arching shrub reaching 5 by 4 ft (1.5 x 1.2 m) with rather dull green leaves but beautiful flowers, large, single and pale pink, shading to primrose yellow in the centre and with amber stamens. A fitful autumn repeat.

'**Golden Wings**' (Shepherd, 1956) A wide, bushy grower attaining 5 ft (1.5 m) in height and carrying more or less continuously clusters of large, single, pale yellow, sweetly scented flowers. Light green leaves, generally healthy.

'**Nevada**' (Dot, 1927) Large, creamy white, semi-double flowers borne with such profusion that they completely obscure the leaves, which are small and rather rounded. A big spreading bush, 6 ft (1.8 m) high and wide, with some second blooming, though not equal to that at midsummer.

'**Roseraie de l'Hay**' (Cochet-Cochet, 1902) The ideal hedging rose, bushy and dense with leaves to the ground and very thorny stems. A Rugosa reaching 6 ft (1.8 m) in height and fine for health. Flowers double and loosely formed, wine-red and with the sweetest fragrance, almost continuous from summer to autumn.

'**Sally Holmes**' (Holmes, 1976) The large, single, creamy white flowers are carried in clusters and are very profuse on a wide-spreading bush that will go up to about 4 ft (1.2 m). A good repeat.

GROUND-COVER ROSES

'**Bonica**' (Meilland, 1982) Forms a dense mound about 3 ft (1 m) high and 4 ft (1.2 m) across and, if closely planted, makes good ground cover. Pale pink, double, cupped flowers and orange hips.

'**Ferdy**' (Keisei, 1984) Clusters of fuchsia-pink flowers with creamy yellow stamens on a wide-spreading bush 4 ft (1.2 m) wide by 3 ft (1 m) high. Attractive, arching growth.

'**Pheasant**' (Kordes, 1986) Trusses of full, deep rose-pink blooms on a prostrate grower that will hug the ground and spread out to about 10 ft (3 m). 'Partridge' and 'Grouse', from the same breeder, are similar. (See p.56.)

'**Pink Bells**' (and 'Red Bells' and 'White Bells') (Poulsen, 1980) The first-rate foliage of these roses densely covers the ground beneath them, spreading to about 4 ft (1.2 m) wide. Height 2 ft (60 cm). Double blooms borne in abundance, but only during July and August. (See p.10.)

R. × paulii 'Rosea' See p.50.

'**Smarty**' (Ilsink, 1979) Clusters of semi-double, light pink blooms on a low-growing, spreading bush with good, glossy foliage. Recurrent. Grows 3 ft (1 m) tall and across.

Opposite: modern shrub roses – 'Constance Spry', 'Cornelia' (top left and right); 'Fru Dagmar Hastrup', 'Golden Wings' (centre left and right); 'Nevada', 'Sally Holmes' (bottom left and right)

Miniature roses – 'Angela Rippon' (left), 'Anna Ford' (right)

MINIATURE ROSES

In these descriptions, tall means 12–15 in. (30–38 cm) and medium 8–12 in. (20–30 cm).

'**Angela Rippon**' (De Ruiter, 1978) Tall, bushy growth. Fairly large, coral-pink blooms.

'**Anna Ford**' (Harkness, 1980) Clusters of deep orange, semi-double blooms on a very bushy plant of medium height.

'**Baby Gold Star**' (Dot, 1940) Large, bright yellow blooms on a bushy plant of medium height.

'**Baby Masquerade**' (Tantau, 1956) Tall, bushy and twiggy, with tiny leaves and flowers in shades of yellow and deep pink like the cluster-flowered parent. No scent.

'**Bit o' Sunshine**' (Moore, 1956) Large, full, light yellow blooms on a fairly tall bush. Disease to be watched for.

'**Fire Princess**' (Moore, 1969) Upright and tall, with clusters of full, scarlet blooms. Good as a cut flower.

'**Lavender Jewel**' (Moore, 1978) Large, very full blooms in pink and lavender blends. Bushy and of medium height. Suitable for cutting.

'**Magic Carrousel**' (Moore, 1972) Medium-sized, rather cupped blooms, white, the petals tipped pink. Upright and bushy, tall. Good cut flower.

'**Peek a Boo**' (Dickson, 1981) Graceful sprays of apricot-pink flowers on a rounded plant that could be classed as a patio rose, as it may reach 18 in. (45 cm).

'**Pompon de Paris**' Climbing version of an early nineteenth-century miniature rose. It will go up 10 ft (3 m) or more, covered in bright pink flowers of informal shape.

'**Red Ace**' (De Ruiter, 1982) Clusters of moderately full, deep crimson blooms. A compact, upright grower of medium height, good for showing.

'**Robin Redbreast**' (Interplant, 1983) Medium to tall, bushy growth carrying semi-double, dark red blooms with a white eye. Slightly fragrant.

'**Stacey Sue**' (Moore, 1976) A tall, bushy, rather lax grower bearing clusters of very double, light pink blooms with great freedom. Good for showing.

'**Starina**' (Meilland, 1965) One of the best, with large, orange-red blooms on a good, sturdy, bushy plant. May grow to 18 in. (45 cm). A winner on the show bench.

Propagation

The easiest way to propagate roses is to take cuttings. Budding or grafting on to rootstocks is quicker but more complicated, and for most amateurs cuttings will provide all the extra plants needed.

It is certainly true that not all roses grow with equal vigour when on their own roots, which they will be if they have been raised from cuttings. This is particularly so with large- and cluster-flowered varieties, which will also give the poorest returns in the cuttings bed. Probably the easiest roses to strike are ramblers, many of the shrub roses and miniatures, the latter being more likely to retain their small size if they are not on rootstocks. Species roses will strike well too, but when on their own roots they tend to make an inordinate amount of new growth at the expense of flowers. In general it could be said that the nearer a rose is to its wild ancestors, the easier it will be to take cuttings from. However, it is worth having a go with any rose, for it is an unpredictable business.

Rose cuttings will be quite happy in the open, provided the bed is in a place with plenty of light but shaded to some extent from the full midday sun. Early autumn is the time to take them, choosing strong, well-ripened shoots from the current season's growth. Those that have borne flowers which are now over should be at just the right stage. Prepare the cuttings as shown in figure 9 (p.56) and then put them in a polythene bag until you are ready to plant them. They should not be allowed to dry out.

The easiest way to prepare for planting, particularly if your soil is light, is to thrust a spade in to a depth of about 6 in. (15 cm) and move it backwards and forwards to create an open slot. This can be repeated until you have the required length of slot, based on the assumption of 4–6 in. (10–15 cm) between each cutting. If your soil is on the heavy side, sprinkle a little coarse sand along the bottom slot, dip your cuttings in hormone rooting powder (which is like taking out insurance, but may not be needed), and then place them upright in the slot so that 6 in. (15 cm) or two thirds of their length is below ground. Tread along the sides of the slot to push the earth back into place and water well.

Keep watering during dry spells and, during the following winter, tread again after frosts in case the cuttings have been loosened in the soil. In spring they should start to make new growth and will probably produce some flower buds. It is best, however, to remove these in the first summer so that the infant plants can devote all their energies to making strong root systems. Looking decorative can come later. You must expect to wait until the autumn, spraying against disease and pests as with other roses during the summer, before you can move them to their final quarters. Even then it will be another year or two before they will be able to claim the status of fully grown plants.

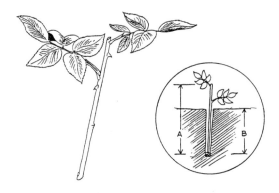

Figure 9: taking a cutting – the cuts in the shoot should be made just above and just below a bud, as shown, and two leaves left at the top; in the small diagram A is 9 in. (23 cm) and B 6 in. (15 cm)

'Partridge', a modern Wichuraiana hybrid, from the same stable as 'Pheasant'

Pests and diseases

There is quite a range of pests that may attack roses, but in most years and in most gardens greenfly (aphids) are the only problem of serious concern to the rose grower. They are the first eleven. The second eleven might consist of caterpillars and, especially in areas sheltered by trees, the leaf-rolling sawfly. The rest are in the reserves, but it is nevertheless useful to be able to identify them so that measures can be taken for their elimination if necessary.

Some pests suck the rose sap and some eat the leaves, and both kinds can be dealt with most effectively with modern chemical sprays. In fact, one spray will often treat a range of pests and, if you spray against greenfly, you will be getting rid of a whole lot of other undesirables at the same time. Again, certain sprays are mixed with fungicides, so that yet another job, protection against fungus attacks, is accomplished simultaneously. These are usually sold ready mixed, and you should never experiment by mixing sprays yourself: not only is this illegal, but you may damage your roses seriously. Systemic sprays have the advantage that the chemical enters the plant tissues and will stay active there for several weeks, the insecticides poisoning sap-suckers and the fungicides preventing disease. These sprays will not be washed off by rain.

Always take great care when using chemical sprays to follow the manufacturer's instructions. It is advisable to wear protective clothing, including rubber gloves, and to wash your hands carefully when you have finished. This is not, it should be stressed, an alarmist doctrine: it is common sense.

Never spray in hot sunshine, when the leaves may be scorched. Early evening, in time to give the plants a chance to dry before dark, is best. Avoid windy days, when the spray might be blown onto something that does not relish it. Do not waste spray, as it is very expensive and getting more so every year. A good general approach is to spray only when you see the first signs of attack, either by insects or by fungus diseases like mildew and black spot. However, if you live in an area where black spot is a serious problem year by year, preventive spraying may be necessary, beginning immediately after spring pruning and repeating at fortnightly intervals. Preventive measures may sometimes be needed in one or two other cases, which are indicated in the table overleaf. With a little vigilance, there is no need nowadays for your roses to be disfigured by pests or disease.

ROSE PESTS

Pest and symptoms	Treatment
Greenfly (aphids) Small green or pale pinkish brown insects clustering thickly on new shoots, buds and under leaves.	Spray with dimethoate, malathion, fenitrothion or pirimiphos-methyl.
Caterpillars All eat leaves causing irregular holes and/or bore into flower buds. Caterpillars of the tortrix moth hide in rolled-up leaves, the edges held together with silken threads. Those of the lackey moth spin silken tents, and those of the winter moth hide between two leaves stuck together. The rose leaf miner is a small moth caterpillar which bores into the leaf tissues, leaving light-coloured, twisting lines on the leaf surfaces.	Remove by hand if the attack is minor and pick off affected leaves. Otherwise spray with fenitrothion, gamma HCH, permethrin or pirimiphos-methyl.
Leaf-rolling sawfly Tiny, black, flying insects. Eggs are laid in the leaf margins and an injected toxin rolls the leaf up longitudinally over the egg and larvae, which are pale green caterpillars. Can be a problem in areas surrounded by trees.(See p.60.)	Preventive spraying with fenitrothion or pirimiphos-methyl in mid-May and again early in June. Once the leaves have rolled, they should be picked off and burned.
Chafers Beetles that nibble rose petals and anthers – the cockchafer, the rose chafer and the garden chafer.	Pick off beetles and spray as for caterpillars.
Froghopper Blobs of froth (cuckoo spit) on shoots and leaf joints, concealing the greenish yellow insect, which sucks sap.	Pick off and destroy with finger and thumb or spray as for greenfly.
Leafhopper White mottling of the leaves and greyish white moulted skins on the undersides, where the nymphs and adults suck sap.	Spray as for aphids.
Red spider mite So small as to be difficult to see. They suck sap, causing yellow dots and patches on the leaves and their minute webs on the undersides can be a tell-tale sign.	So far, there is little real control. Frequent cold water sprays or a systemic insecticide may make some difference.
Rose slugworm Slug-like, greenish yellow caterpillars with pale brown heads graze leaf surfaces, which develop skeletal brown patches.	Spray with malathion, permethrin or gamma HCH.
Scale insects Female insects and eggs are hidden under brown limpet-like scales on the rose stem.	Spray with dimethoate, pirimiphos-methyl or malathion in early July.

ROSE PESTS (continued)

Pest and symptoms	**Treatment**
Thrips Tiny, sap-sucking insects which can be damaging in hot weather. They leave buds and flowers ragged-looking with discoloured petals.	Spray as for aphids.

ROSE DISEASES

Disease and symptoms	**Treatment**
Black spot Airborne spores cause rounded black spots on the leaves, which quickly spread. The leaves turn yellow and eventually drop off, over a time seriously weakening the plant. Usually attacks the lower, older leaves first and spreads rapidly.(See p.60.)	Spray with benomyl, carbendazim, triforine, bupirimate-triforine, thiophanate-methyl or fenarimol. Remove and burn affected leaves.
Canker Brown, cracked, sunken areas on rose shoots where damage to the shoot has allowed the entry of disease spores.	Cut the shoot below affected area. Disinfect secateurs afterwards with methylated spirit.
Mildew Airborne spores causing greyish white powdery-looking covering on rose leaves and flower stalks. Spreads quickly and leads to distorted growth. (See p.60.)	Spray as for black spot.
Rose rust Orange spots on undersides of leaves, later turning black and eventually resulting in defoliation.(See p.60.)	Spray with myclobutanil, triforine or propiconazole.
Die-back Shoots dying back from the tip, becoming brown and wrinkled. Caused by the fungus *Botrytis cinerea*.	Cut back shoots to healthy tissue.

One final word. Strong, well-cared for roses are less likely to be seriously troubled by pests and diseases, so the better you look after them the less spraying you will have to do.

Pests and diseases – above: leaf-rolling sawfly (left), black spot (right); below: mildew (left), rust (right)

Further information

ROSES WITH DECORATIVE AUTUMN HIPS

R. *glauca* (R. *rubrifolia*)
R. *moyesii* and 'Geranium' and R. 'Highdownensis'
R. *multibracteata*
R. *rubiginosa* (R. *eglanteria*) and its Penzance Brier hybrids
R. *rugosa* 'Alba', 'Rubra', 'Scabrosa' and 'Fru Dagmar Hastrup'
R. 'Scarlet Fire'
R. 'Wolley-Dod' R. *villosa* (R. *pomifera*) 'Duplex'
R. *sweginzowii*
R. *webbiana*

The bright red hips of *Rosa glauca* contrast pleasantly with the
purplish grey foliage

STRONGLY SCENTED ROSES

While all these roses can be considered highly scented, it should not be forgotten that fragrance can vary markedly from day to day, or even during the course of one day, according to temperature and humidity. Individual people vary, too, in the amount of fragrance they can detect.

Large-flowered roses

'Alec's Red'	'Loving Memory'	'Royal Highness'
'Alpine Sunset'	'Mala Rubinstein'	'Solitaire'
'Blue Moon'	'Mary Donaldson'	'Sutter's Gold'
'Deep Secret'	'Mister Lincoln'	'Sweetheart'
'Dutch Gold'	'My Choice'	'Tenerife'
'Ernest H. Morse'	'My Love'	'The Coxwain'
'Forgotten Dreams'	'Papa Meilland'	'Velvet Hour'
'Fragrant Cloud'	'Paul Shirville'	'Wendy Cussons'
'Johnnie Walker'	'Pristine'	'Whisky Mac'

Cluster-flowered roses

'Arthur Bell'	'Escapade'	'Orange Sensation'
'Avocet'	'Fragrant Delight'	'Radox Bouquet'
'Beauty Queen'	'Harry Edland'	'Scented Air'
'Dearest'	'Iceberg'	'Sheila's Perfume'
'Deb's Delight'	'Korresia'	'Shocking Blue'
'Elizabeth of Glamis'	'Margaret Merril'	'Southampton'
'English Miss'	'Memento'	'Yvonne Rabier'

Climbers and ramblers

'Albertine'	'Coral Dawn'	'Maigold'
'Aloha'	'Dreaming Spires'	'New Dawn'
'Bobbie James'	'Francis E. Lester'	'Wedding Day'
'Breath of Life'	'Guinée'	
'Compassion'	'Highfield'	

GARDENS WITH ROSE COLLECTIONS

(NT = National Trust)

Arley Hall, Northwich, Cheshire (mainly old roses)
Castle Howard, North Yorks (old)
Chester Zoo, Chester (modern roses)
Dixon Park, Belfast (both old and modern)
Duthie Park, Aberdeen (modern)
The Gardens of the Rose (Royal National Rose Society), St Albans, Herts (both)
Gunby Hall (NT), Spilsby, Lincs (mainly old)

The famous rambler 'Albertine' (left) is still prized for its abundance of fragrant blooms; the large, shapely flowers of 'Fantin Latour' (right) are strongly scented

Haddon Hall, Bakewell, Derbys (mainly modern)
Hatfield House, Hatfield, Herts (mainly old)
Hampton Court Palace, Hampton Court, Surrey (modern)
Heale House, Middle Woodford, Wilts (mainly old)
Hidcote Manor (NT), Chipping Camden, Glos (old)
Hyde Hall, Rettendon, Essex (both)
Kiftsgate Court, Chipping Camden, Glos (old)
Mannington Hall, Saxthorpe, Norfolk (old)
Mottisfont Abbey (NT), Romsey, Hants (old)
Newby Hall, Ripon, North Yorks (mainly old)
Nymans (NT), Handcross, West Sussex (old)
Oxford Botanic Gardens, Oxford (old)
Polesden Lacey (NT), Dorking, Surrey (both)
Queen Mary's Garden, Regent's Park, London (both)
Saughton Park, Edinburgh (modern)
Sissinghurst Castle (NT), Sissinghurst, Kent (old)
Syon Park, Brentford, Middlesex (mainly modern)
Wisley Garden (Royal Horticultural Society), Woking, Surrey (both)

ROSE NURSERIES

Anderson's Rose Nurseries, Friarsfield Rd, Cults, Aberdeen
Apuldram Roses, Apuldram Lane, Dell Quay, Chichester, West Sussex
David Austin Roses, Bowling Green Lane, Albrighton, Wolverhampton
Peter Beales Roses, London Rd, Attleborough, Norfolk

Cants of Colchester Ltd, Nyland Rd, Colchester, Essex
James Cocker & Sons, Whitemyres, Lang Stracht, Aberdeen
Fryers Nurseries Ltd, Manchester Rd, Knutsford, Cheshire
Gandy's Roses Ltd, North Kilworth, Lutterworth, Leics
Gregory's Roses, The Rose Gardens, Stapleford, Nottingham
R. Harkness & Co Ltd, The Rose Gardens, Cambridge Rd, Hitchin, Herts
F. Haynes & Partners Ltd, 56 Gordon St, Kettering, Northants
Highfields Nurseries, Whitminster, Glos
Hillier Nurseries (Winchester) Ltd, Ampfield House, Ampfield, Romsey, Hants
Hill Park Nurseries, Kingston By-Pass, Surbiton, Surrey
C. & K. Jones, Golden Fields Nursery, Barrow Lane, Tarvin, Chester
E. B. Le Grice (Roses) Ltd, Norwich Rd, North Walsham, Norfolk
John Mattock Ltd, The Rose Nurseries, Nuneham Courtenay, Oxford
Notcutts Nurseries Ltd, Woodbridge, Suffolk
Rearsby Roses Ltd, Melton Rd, Rearsby, Leics
Rosemary Roses, The Nurseries, Stapleford Lane, Toton, Beeston, Notts
John Sanday (Roses) Ltd, Over Lane, Almondsbury, Bristol
Sealand Nurseries Ltd, Sealand, Chester, Cheshire
Henry Street, Swallowfield Road Nursery, Arborfield, Reading, Berks
Stydd Nursery, Stonygate Lane, Ribchester, Preston, Lancs
Timmermans Roses, Lowdham Lane, Woodborough, Notts
Warley Rose Gardens Ltd, Warley St, Great Warley, Brentwood, Essex

SOCIETIES

The National Trust, 36 Queen Anne's Gate, London SW1H 9AS. Has many gardens with fine displays of roses, particularly the older varieties.

The Royal Horticultural Society, Vincent Square, Westminster, London SW1P 2PE. The Society's Garden at Wisley in Surrey displays a fine range of roses, both old and new, and roses feature in many of the Society's shows, including Chelsea Show.

The Royal National Rose Society, Chiswell Green, St Albans, Herts AL2 3NR. The Society to which all rose-lovers should belong offers an unrivalled service of information on rose-growing in all its aspects, rose shows in various parts of the country, regular publications for members, and free admission at all times for members to the Society's Gardens of the Rose, which surround the headquarters building near St Albans.